About me

My name is: ____________________

I am in Year: ____________________

Track your progress

As you complete pages in this book, trace over the matching letter here.

OXFORD UNIVERSITY PRESS

d g q

e o

WELL DONE

z h k

n

t i

w b

TOP WORK

Before you begin writing ...

Here are the 3Ps that will help you with your writing: posture, pencil grip and paper position. You will be reminded about these as you work through the book.

Posture

- Relax your arms.
- Sit back in your chair.
- Make sure your back is straight.

Put your feet flat on the floor.

Pencil grip

How you hold your pencil is important.

- Hold your pencil firmly between your thumb and index finger.
- Balance the pencil on your middle finger.
- Don't grip the pencil too tightly!

Left-handed

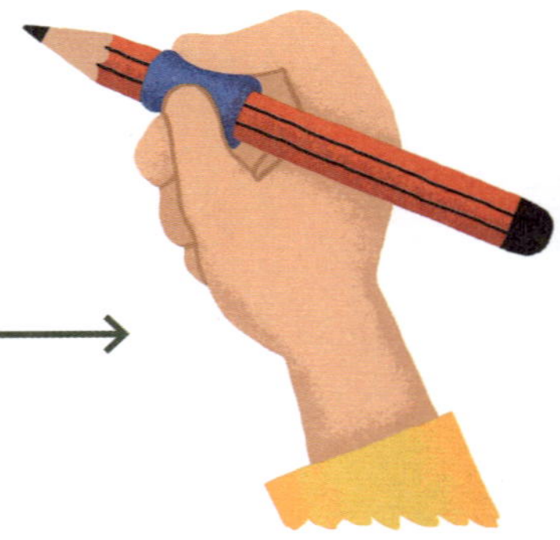

Right-handed

Paper position

- Tilt your page.
- Use your non-writing hand to steady the paper.

Left-handed

Right-handed

Hand and finger warm-ups

Crocodile snaps (whole arms)

Start with one arm straight above your head and the other extended down one side of your body. Snap your hands together, like a crocodile snapping its jaws. Repeat, with your other arm above your head.

Open, shut them. (hands)

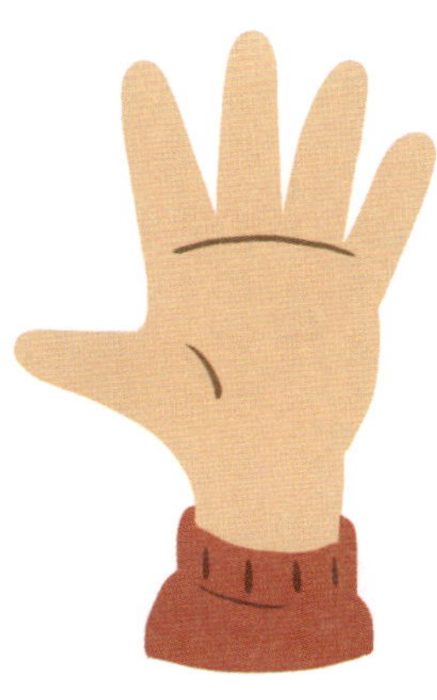

Open, shut them. Open, shut them.
Give a little clap.
Open, shut them. Open, shut them.
Lay them in your lap.
Repeat.

Spider push-ups (fingers)

Place your fingertips together. Bend and straighten your fingers while pushing your fingertips against each other.

Warm-up patterns

Trace the grey lines.

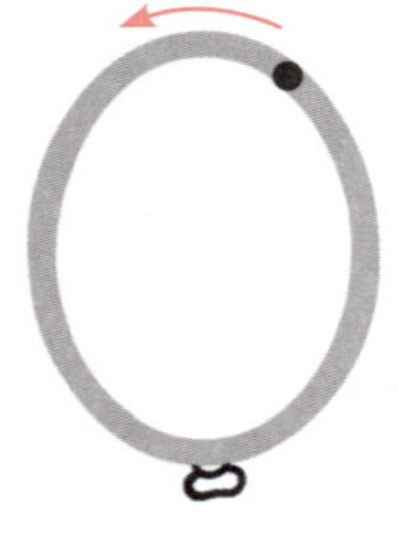

Trace the grey lines.

Have you checked your posture, pencil grip and paper position?

Have you done your warm-ups?

Track, trace and copy the letters and words.

ant

a a a a a a a

a

an am and as ant

an

ark arm art ash

ark

Trace.

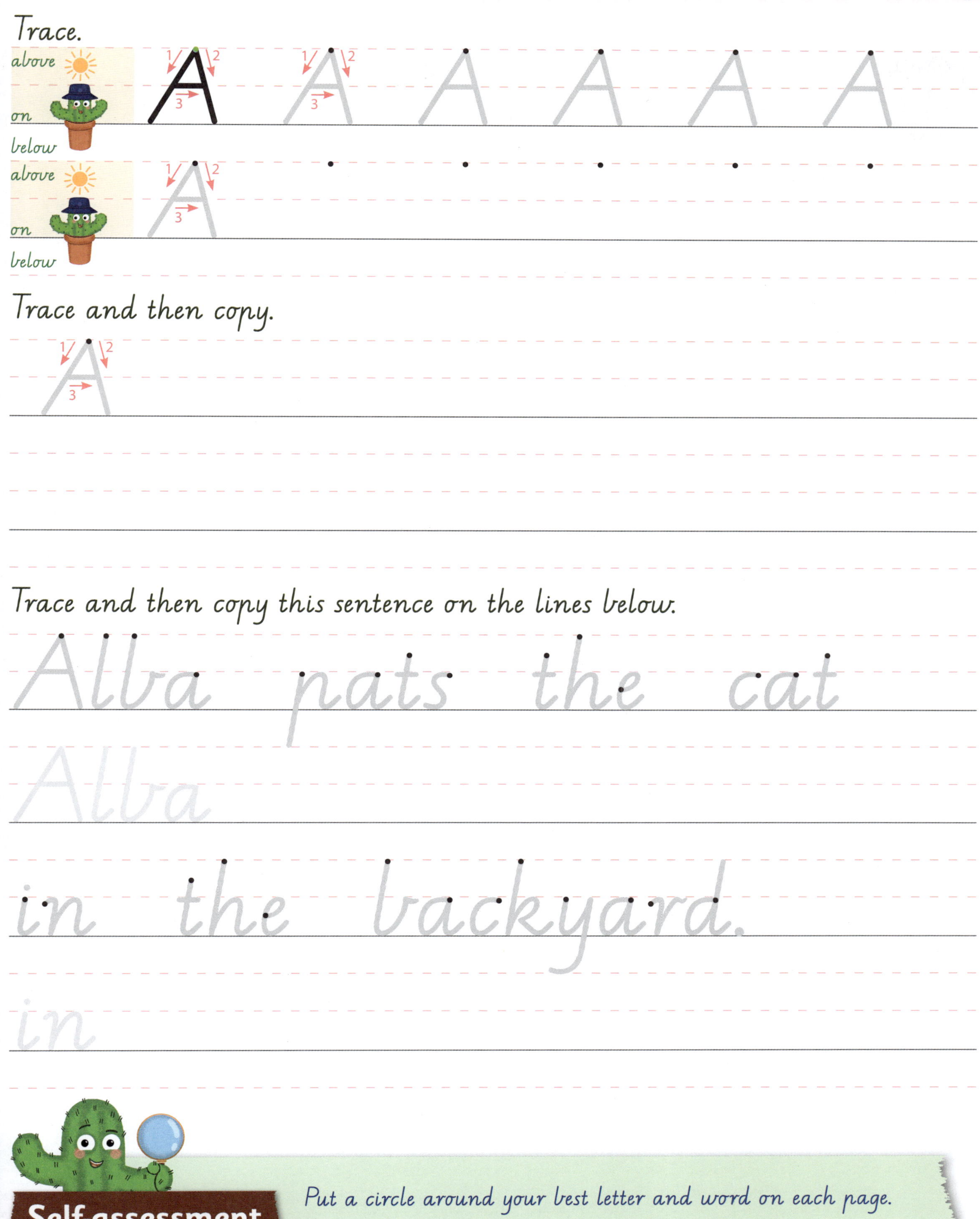

Trace and then copy.

Trace and then copy this sentence on the lines below.

Alba pats the cat

Alba

in the backyard.

in

Self-assessment

Put a circle around your best letter and word on each page.
Explain your choice to your teacher or classmate.

Have you checked your posture, pencil grip and paper position?

Have you done your warm-ups?

c c c

clouds

Track, trace and copy the letters and words.

c c c c c c c

c c c c c c c

c

can cool cats car carpet

can

curl cap card cup cub

curl

Trace.

Trace and then copy.

Trace and then copy this sentence on the lines below.

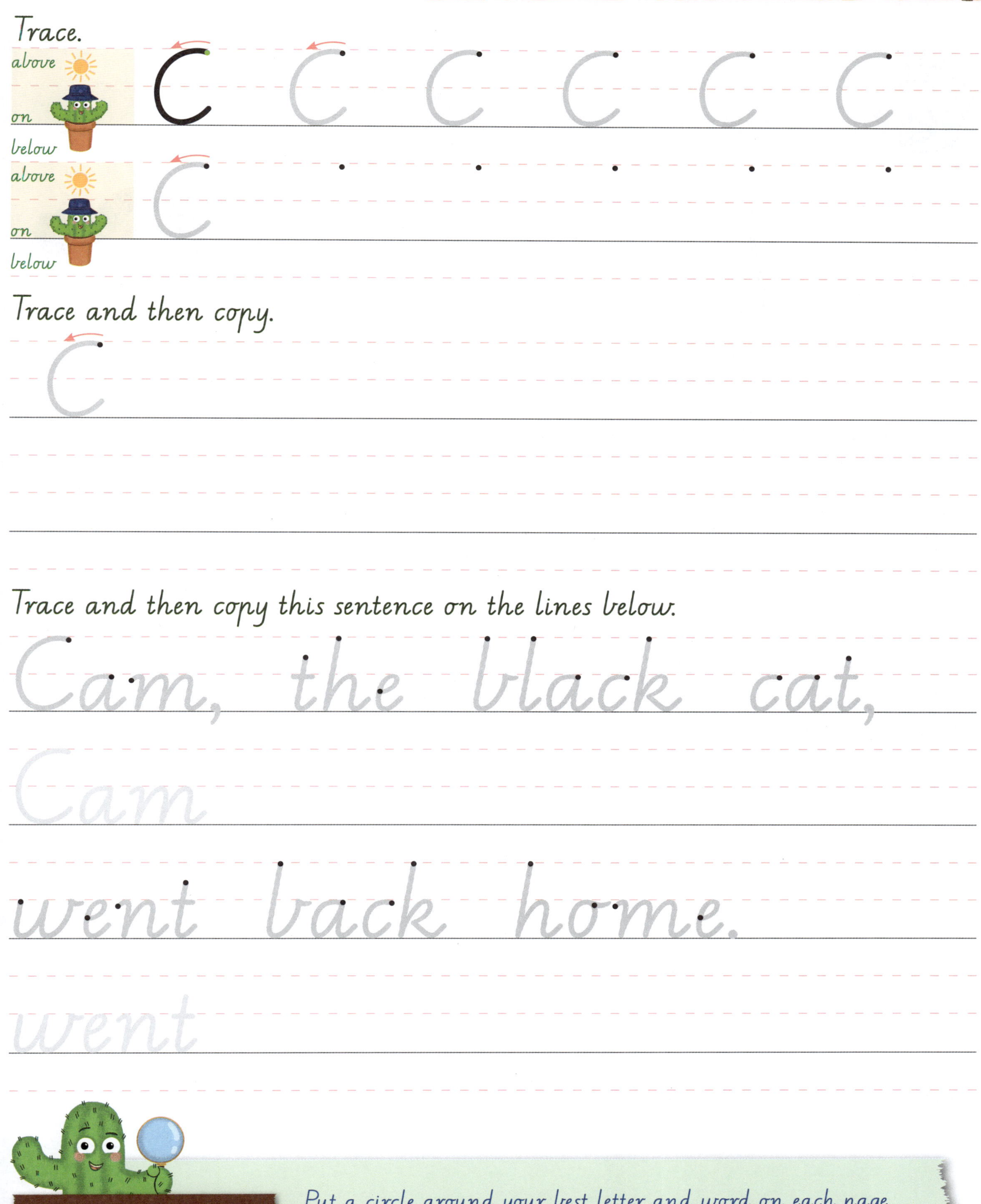

Self-assessment

Put a circle around your best letter and word on each page.
Explain your choice to your teacher or classmate.

Have you checked your posture, pencil grip and paper position?

Have you done your warm-ups?

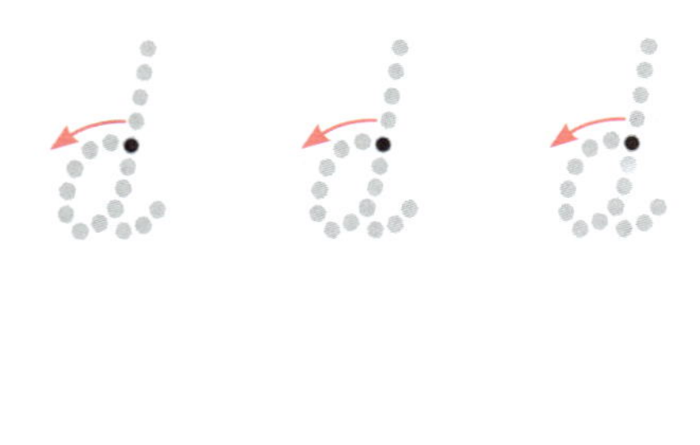

Track, trace and copy the letters and words.

d d d d d d d

d

did dog doll dash dot

did

dig dip dish do dark

dig

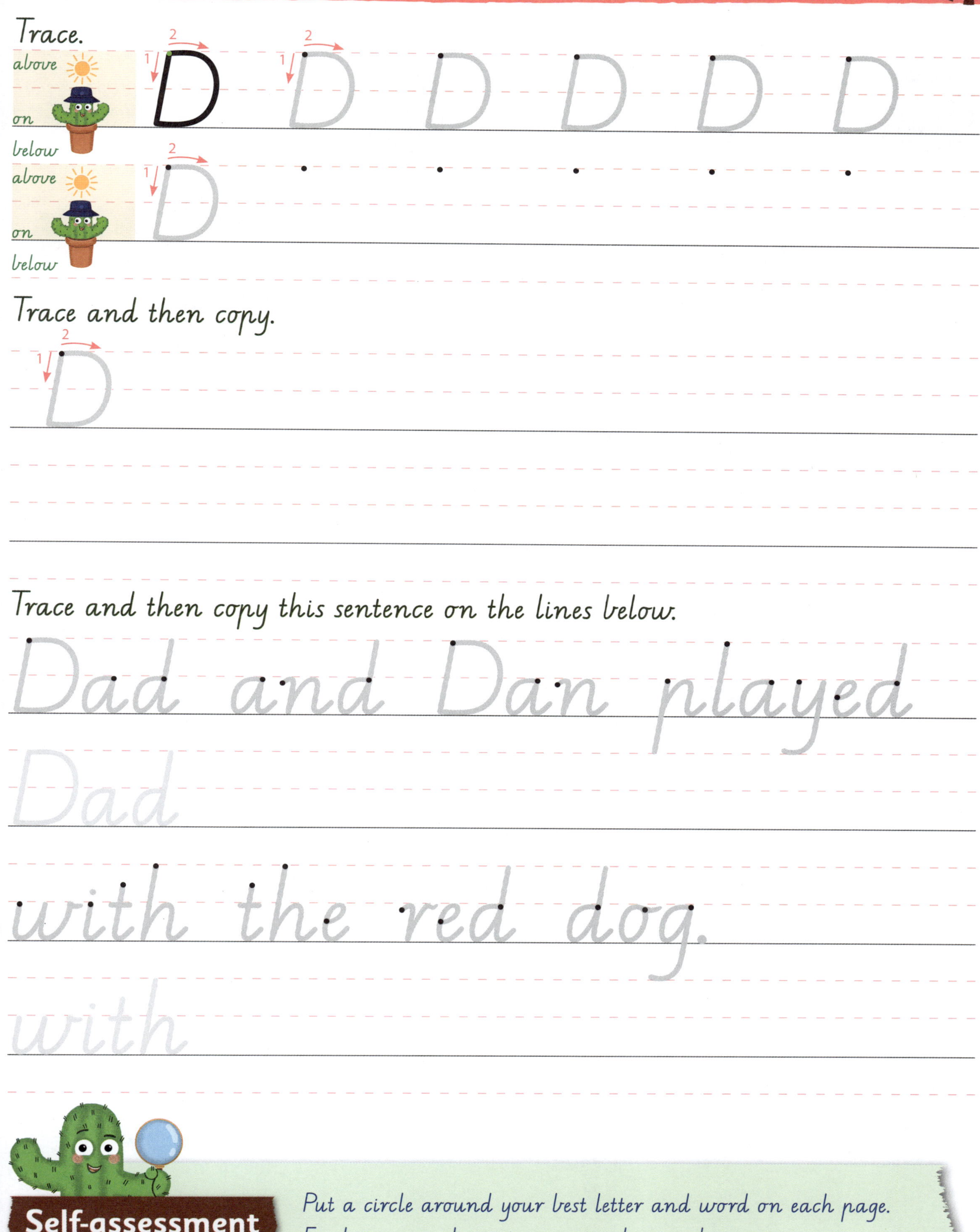

Self-assessment

Put a circle around your best letter and word on each page.
Explain your choice to your teacher or classmate.

Have you checked your posture, pencil grip and paper position?

Have you done your warm-ups?

grandma

Track, trace and copy the letters and words.

g g g g g g g

g g g g g g g

g

got good get grandma

got

gather goat gum giggle

gather

Trace.

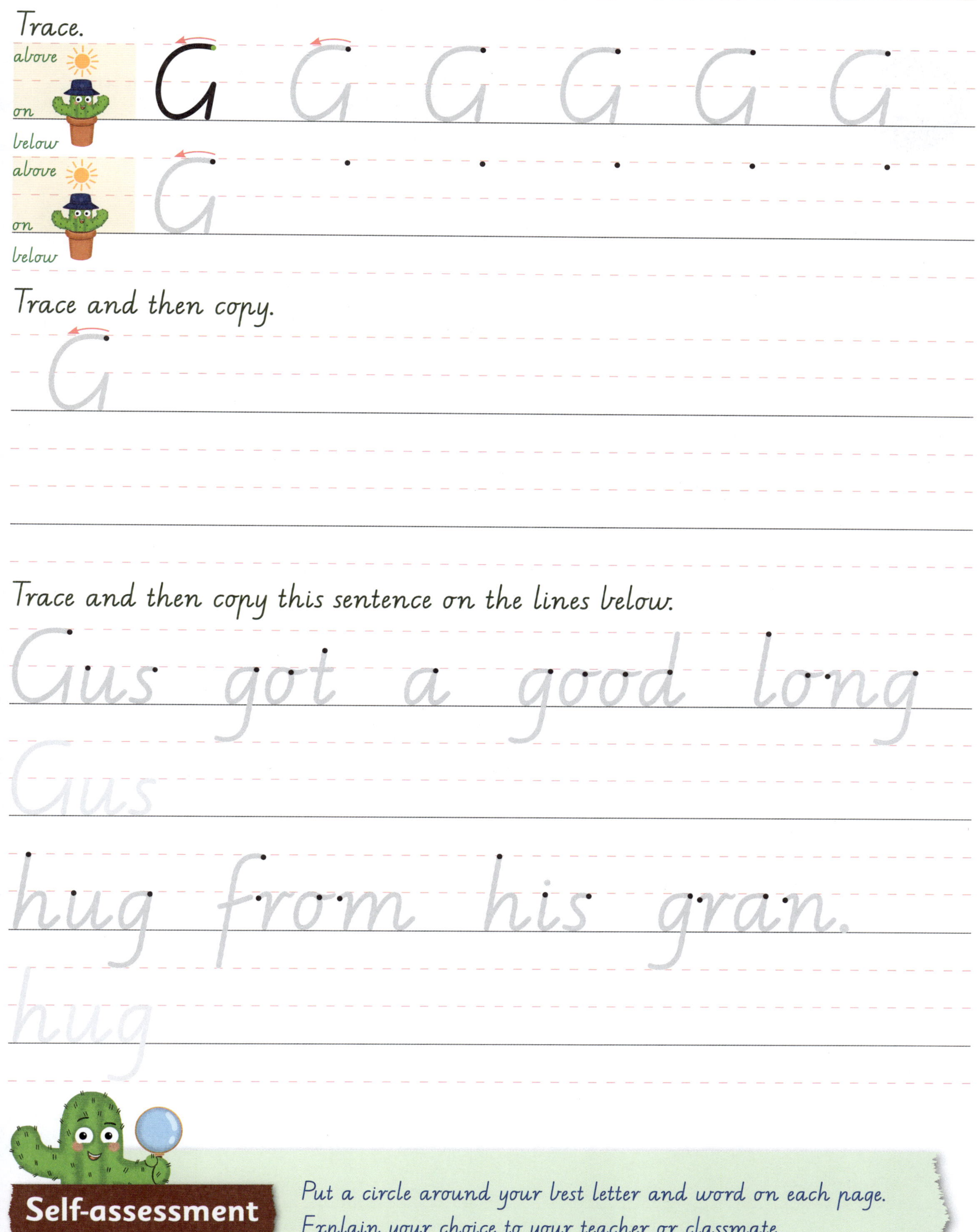

Trace and then copy.

Trace and then copy this sentence on the lines below.

Self-assessment

Put a circle around your best letter and word on each page.
Explain your choice to your teacher or classmate.

Have you checked your posture, pencil grip and paper position?

Have you done your warm-ups?

q q q

quack

Track, trace and copy the letters and words.

q q q q q q q

q q q q q q q

q

quiz quack queen quit

quiz

quick quicker quickest

quick

Trace.

Trace and then copy.

Trace and then copy this sentence on the lines below.

Quin the duck quacks

Quin

near the little pond.

near

Self-assessment

Put a circle around your best letter and word on each page.
Explain your choice to your teacher or classmate.

3Ps Have you checked your posture, pencil grip and paper position?

Have you done your warm-ups?

egg

Track, trace and copy the letters and words.

e e e e e e e

e

egg eggs eve eel end

egg

ear ears exit ever

ear

Trace.

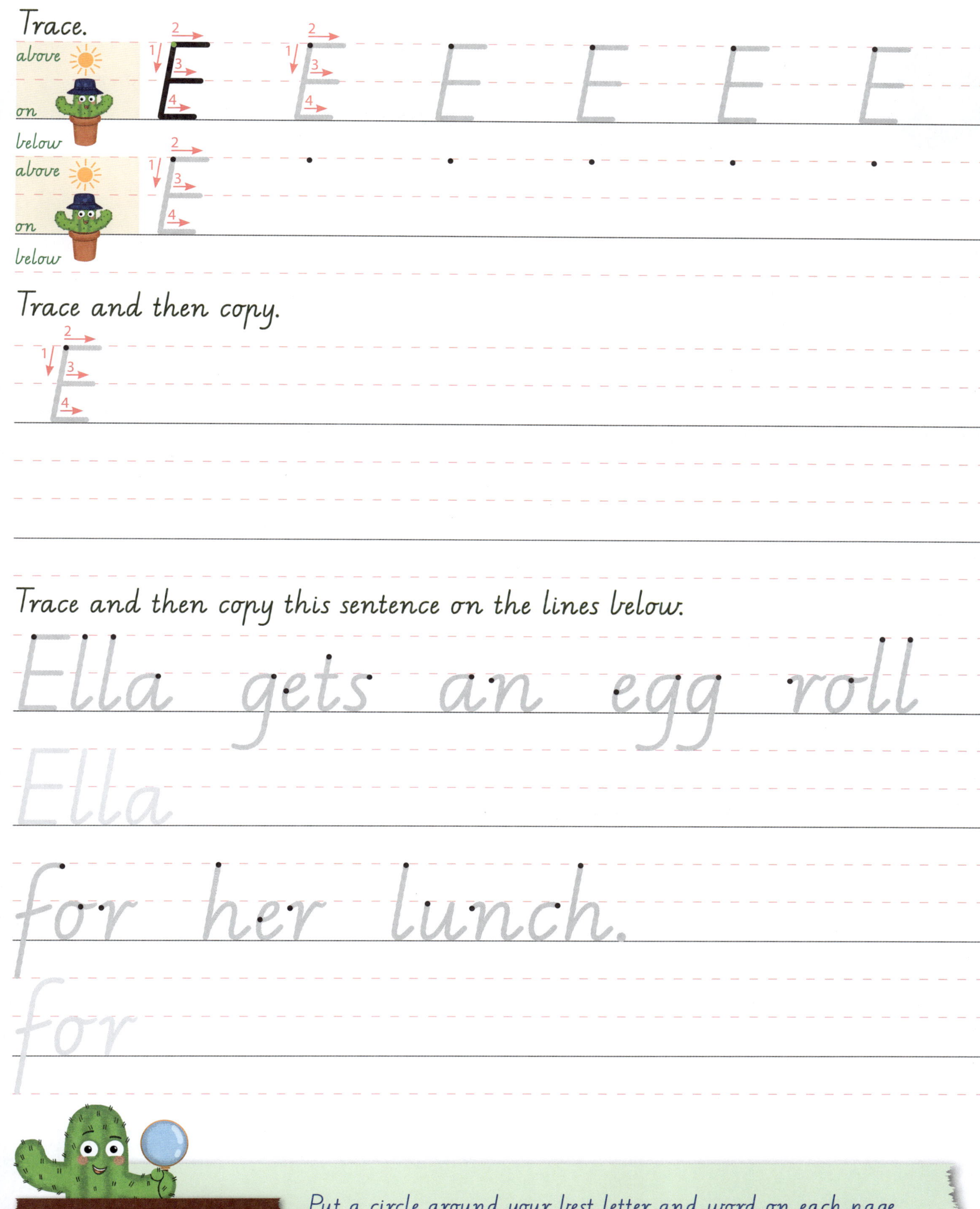

Trace and then copy.

E

Trace and then copy this sentence on the lines below.

Ella gets an egg roll

Ella

for her lunch.

for

Self-assessment

Put a circle around your best letter and word on each page.
Explain your choice to your teacher or classmate.

Have you checked your posture, pencil grip and paper position?

Have you done your warm-ups?

  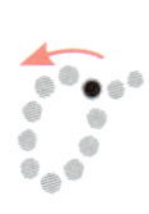

outside

Track, trace and copy the letters and words.

o o o o o o o

o o o o o o o

o

on of order odd

on

oil owl off oats

oil

Self-assessment

Put a circle around your best letter and word on each page. Explain your choice to your teacher or classmate.

Have you checked your posture, pencil grip and paper position?

Have you done your warm-ups?

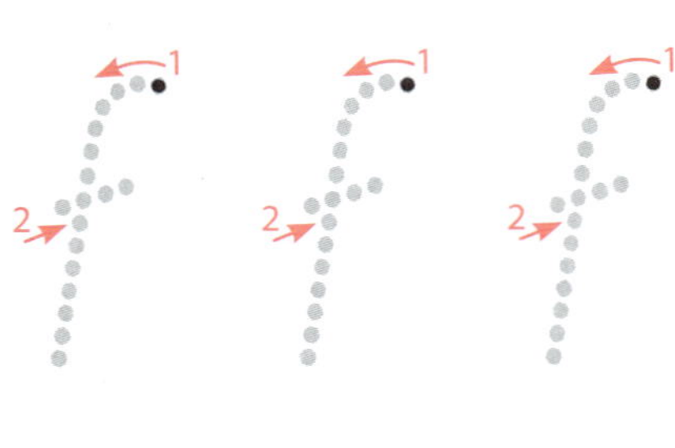

food

Track, trace and copy the letters and words.

f f f f f f f

f f f f f f f

f

fell fun food from

fell

farm fluff feet feed

farm

Trace.

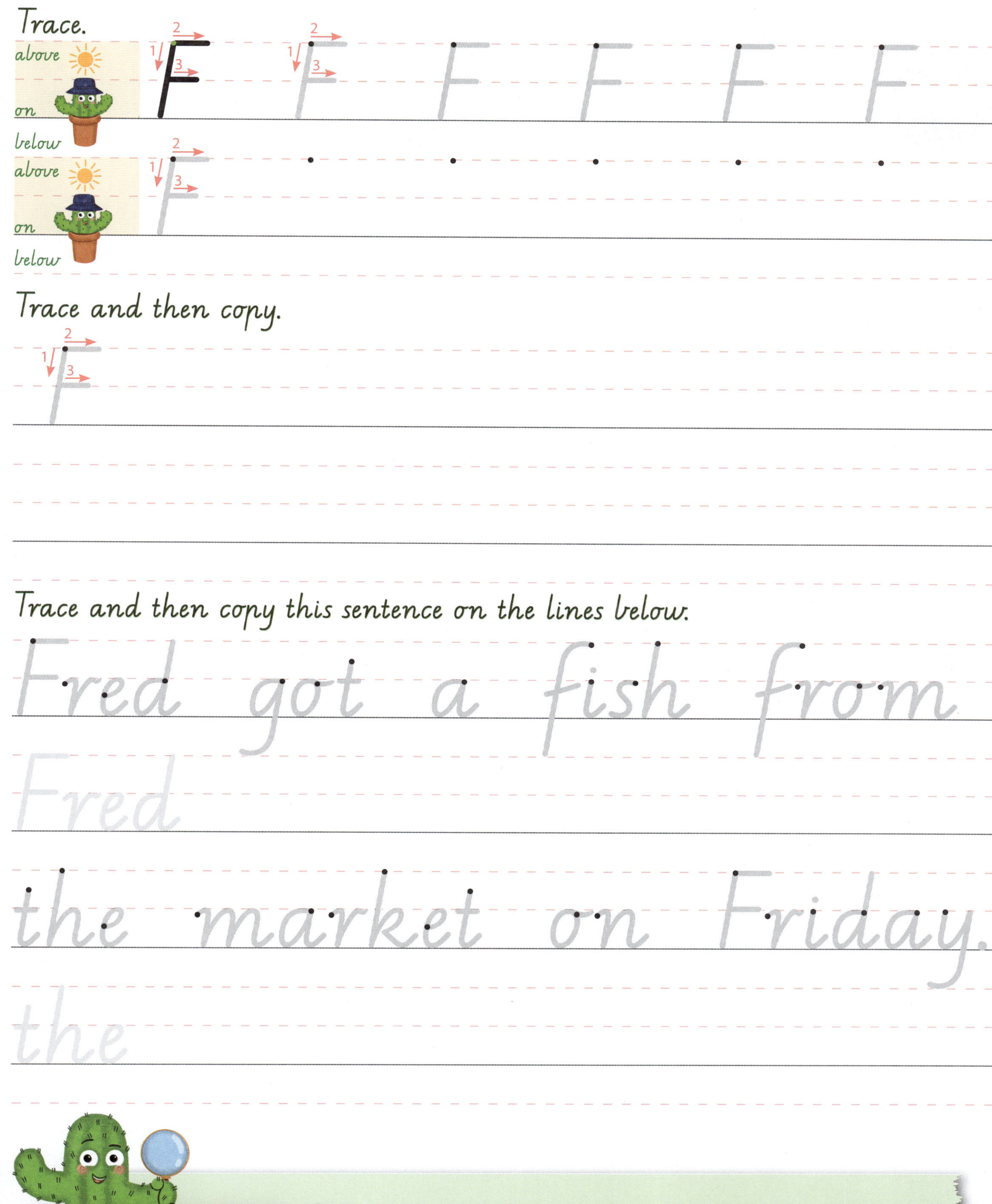

Self-assessment

Put a circle around your best letter and word on each page.
Explain your choice to your teacher or classmate.

3Ps Have you checked your posture, pencil grip and paper position?

Have you done your warm-ups?

s s s

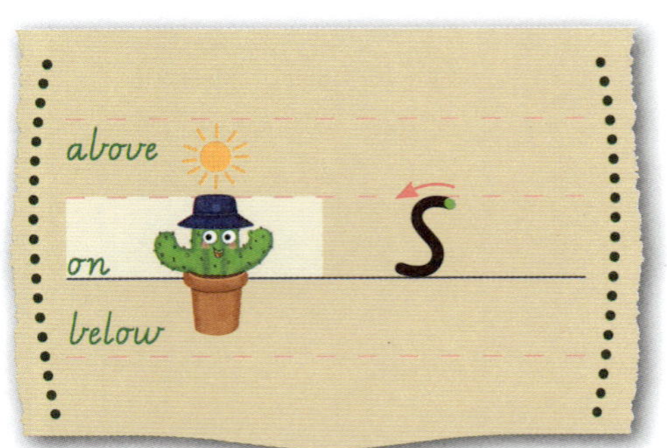

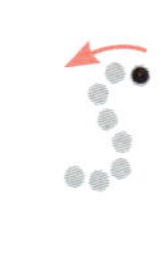

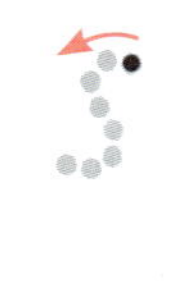

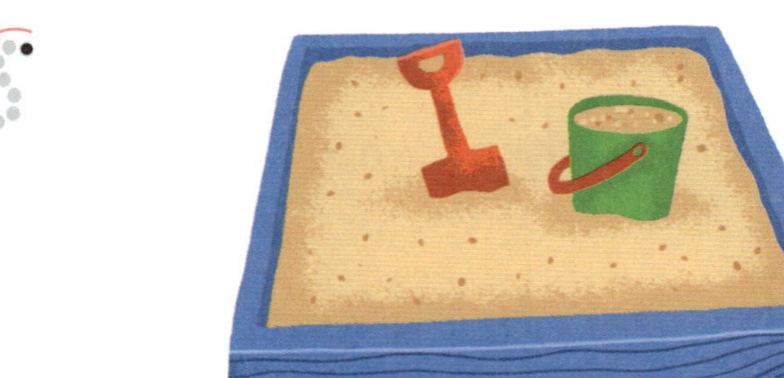

sand

Track, trace and copy the letters and words.

s s s s s s s

s s s s s s s

s

sort sheep shin shed

sort

ships shock strong

ships

Trace.

Trace and then copy.

Trace and then copy this sentence on the lines below.

Sid and Sam sit on the

Sid

sand and sort shells.

sand

Self-assessment

Put a circle around your best letter and word on each page.
Explain your choice to your teacher or classmate.

Have you checked your posture, pencil grip and paper position?

Have you done your warm-ups?

mess

Track, trace and copy the letters and words.

m m m m m m m

m m m m m m m

m

man map mess mum

man

miss mill moon main

miss

OXFORD UNIVERSITY PRESS

Trace.

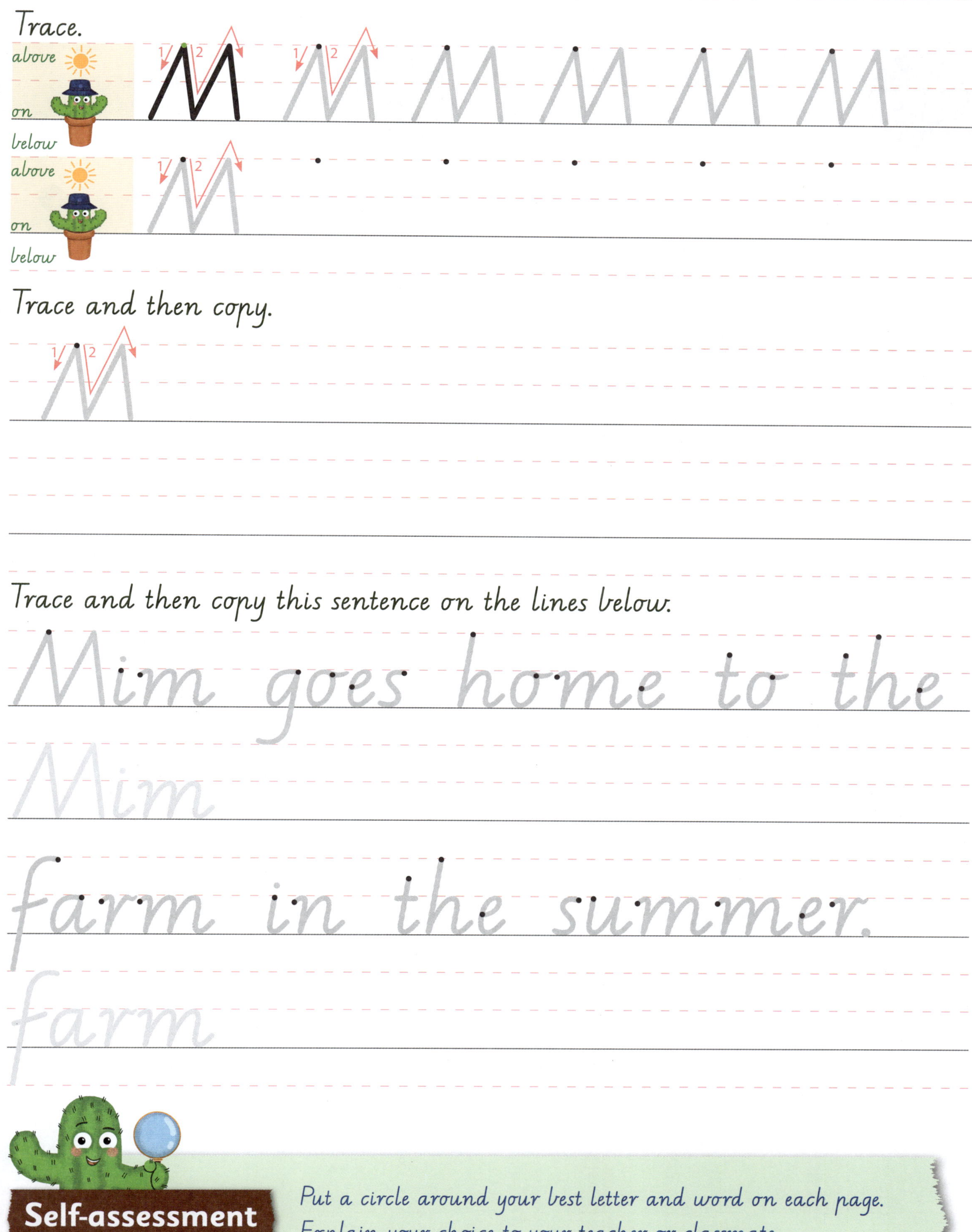

Trace and then copy.

Trace and then copy this sentence on the lines below.

Mim goes home to the

Mim

farm in the summer.

farm

Self-assessment

Put a circle around your best letter and word on each page.
Explain your choice to your teacher or classmate.

Have you checked your posture, pencil grip and paper position?

Have you done your warm-ups?

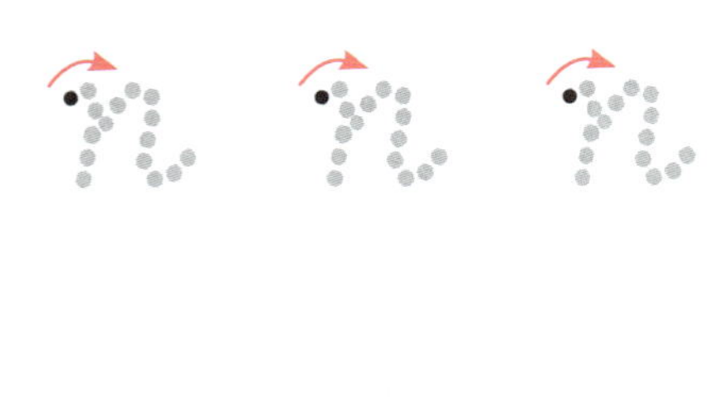

note

Track, trace and copy the letters and words.

n n n n n n n

n n n n n n n

n

not next net near

not

nail nip note nod

nail

Trace.

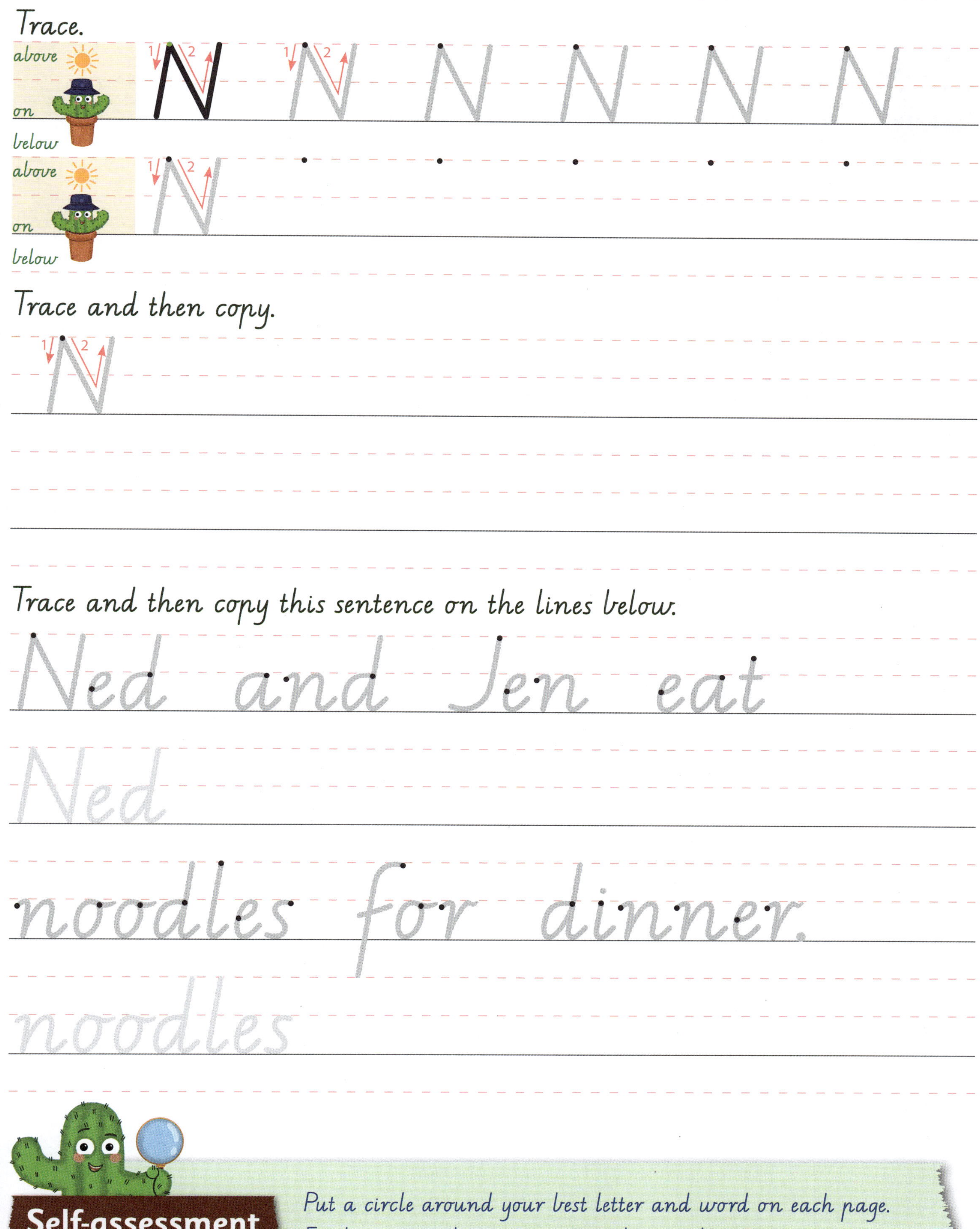

Trace and then copy.

N

Trace and then copy this sentence on the lines below.

Ned and Jen eat

Ned

noodles for dinner.

noodles

Self-assessment

Put a circle around your best letter and word on each page.
Explain your choice to your teacher or classmate.

Have you checked your posture, pencil grip and paper position?

Have you done your warm-ups?

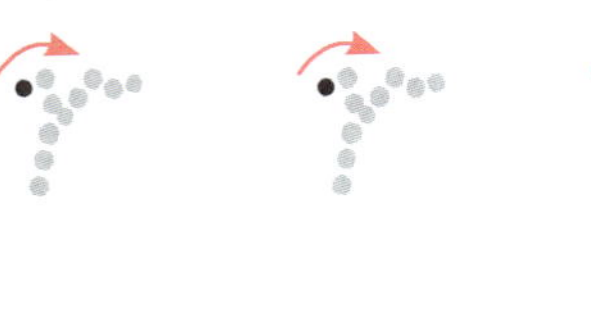

Track, trace and copy the letters and words.

r r r r r r r

r

ran run red rocket

ran

rat reed reef rash rug

rat

OXFORD UNIVERSITY PRESS

Trace.

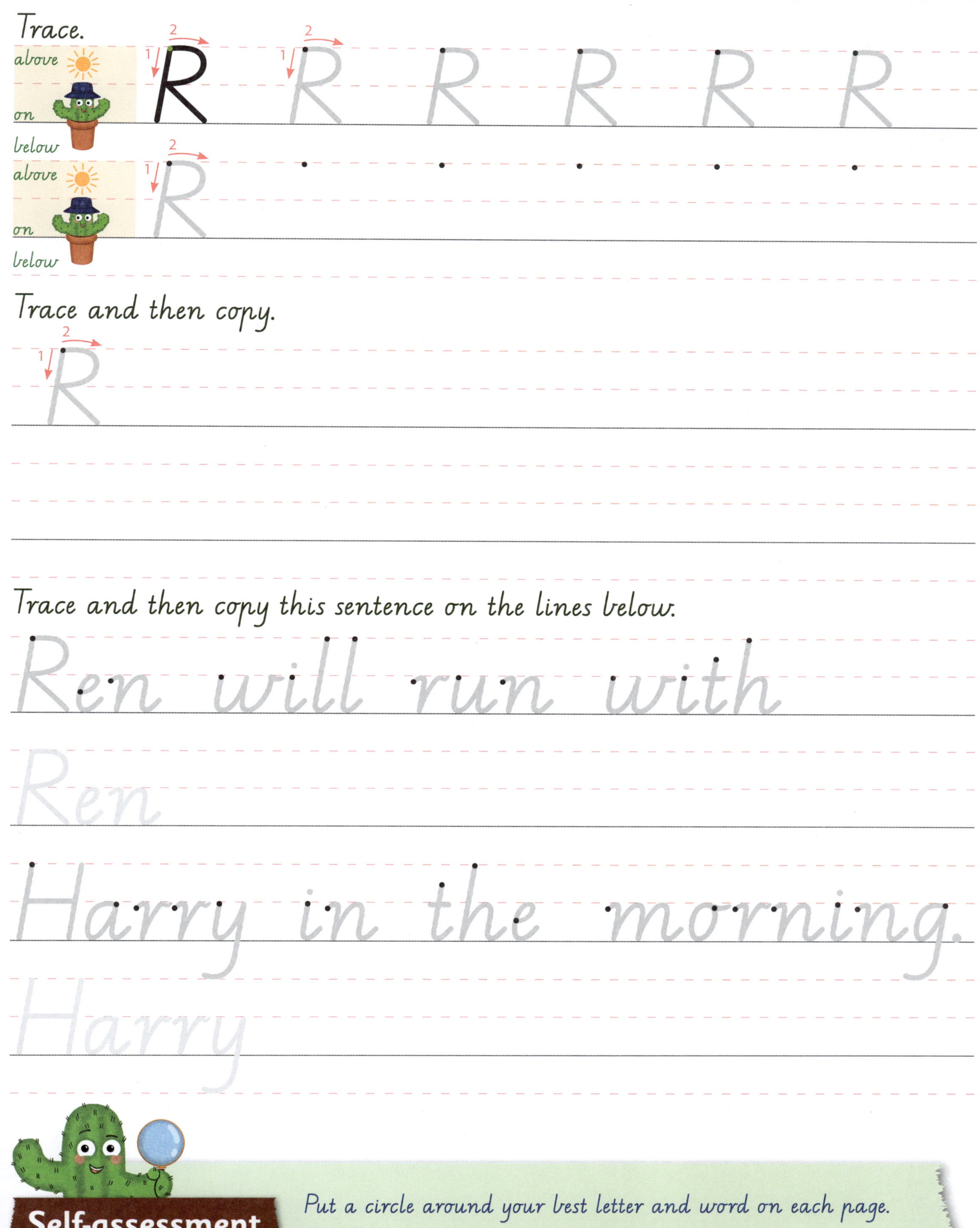

Trace and then copy.

R

Trace and then copy this sentence on the lines below.

Ren will run with

Ren

Harry in the morning.

Harry

Self-assessment

Put a circle around your best letter and word on each page. Explain your choice to your teacher or classmate.

Have you checked your posture, pencil grip and paper position?

Have you done your warm-ups?

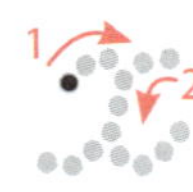 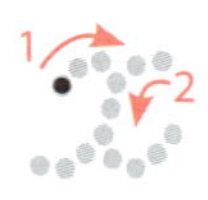 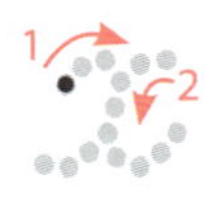

x as in "box"

Track, trace and copy the letters and words.

 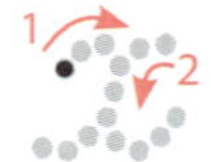 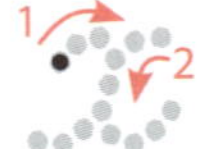 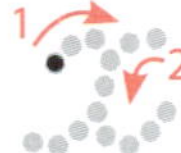   

x x x x x x x

x

box six mix wax text

box

relax taxi fox exit

relax

Trace.

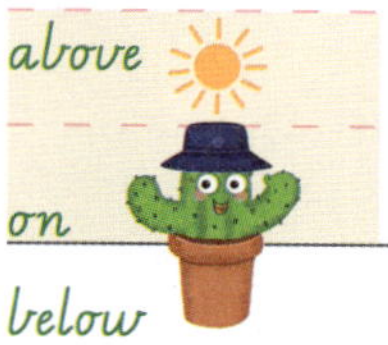
above
on
below

x x x x x x

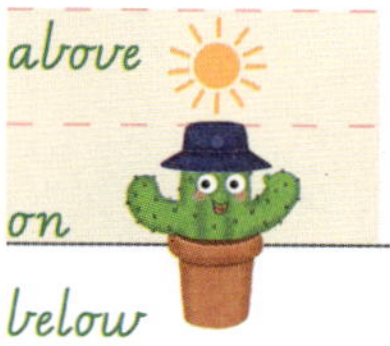
above
on
below

x

Trace and then copy.

x

Trace and then copy this sentence on the lines below.

Xander the ox sat on

Xander

the blue box with a fox.

the

Self-assessment

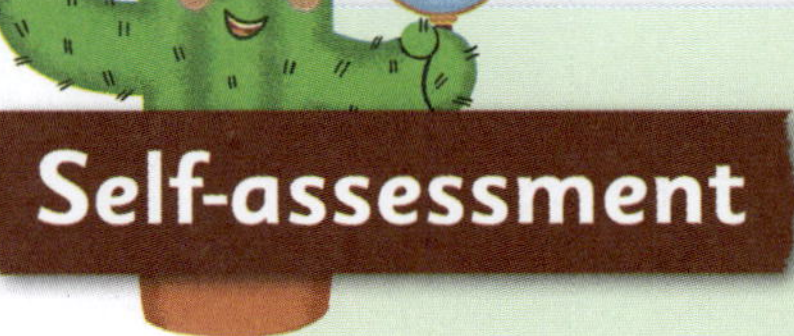

Put a circle around your best letter and word on each page.
Explain your choice to your teacher or classmate.

Have you checked your posture, pencil grip and paper position?

Have you done your warm-ups?

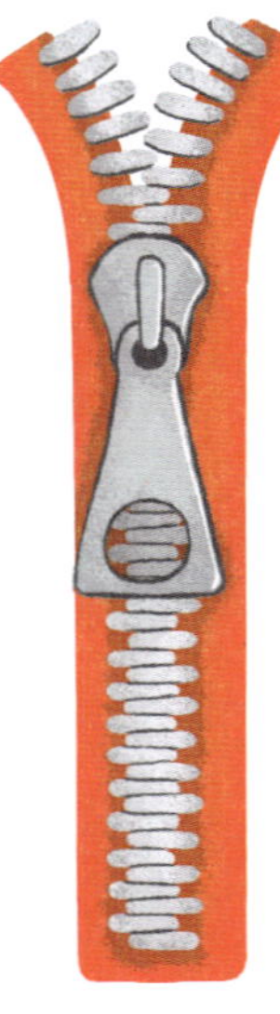

zip

Track, trace and copy the letters and words.

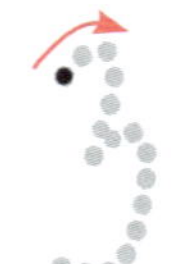

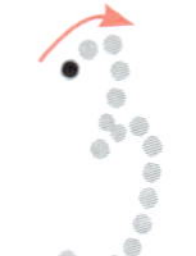

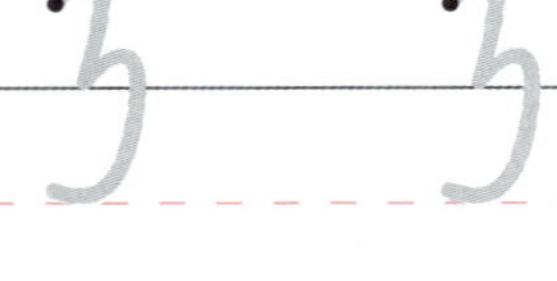

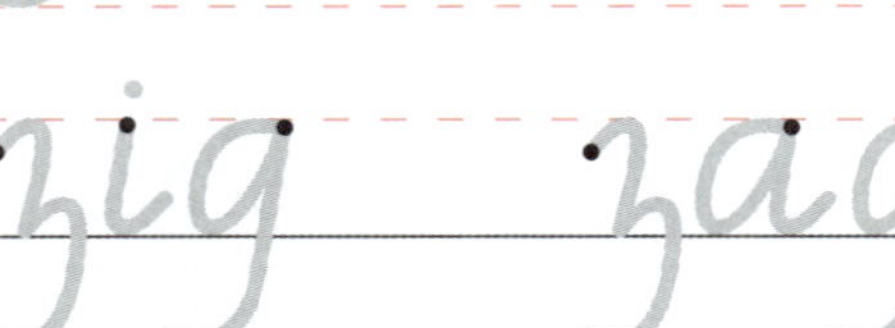

zig zag zap zoom

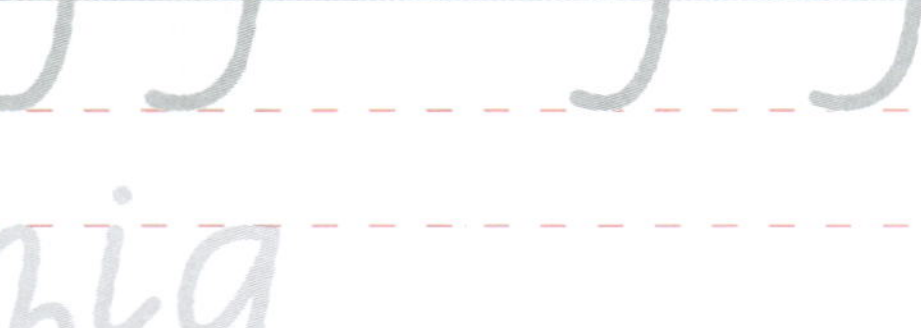

zig

zoo zoos zip buzz

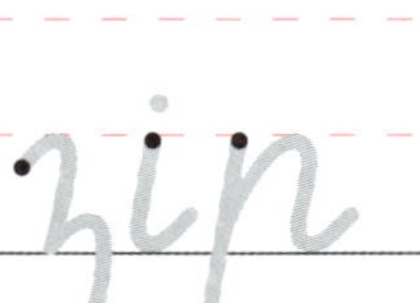

zoo

Self-assessment

Put a circle around your best letter and word on each page.
Explain your choice to your teacher or classmate.

Have you checked your posture, pencil grip and paper position?

Have you done your warm-ups?

h h h

Track, trace and copy the letters and words.

h h h h h h h

h h h h h h h

h

had hot his hammer

had

hair hard hiss heel

hair

OXFORD UNIVERSITY PRESS

Trace.

above
on
below

H H H H H H

above
on
below

H

Trace and then copy.

H

Trace and then copy this sentence on the lines below.

Hank has packed his

Hank

hat for his holiday.

hat

Self-assessment

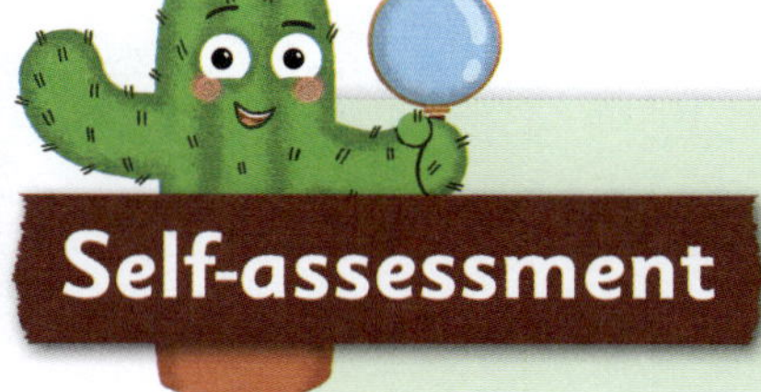

Put a circle around your best letter and word on each page.
Explain your choice to your teacher or classmate.

Have you checked your posture, pencil grip and paper position?

Have you done your warm-ups?

k k k

Track, trace and copy the letters and words.

k k k k k k k

k k k k k k k

k

kit king kittens key

kit

keep kids kick kiss

keep

OXFORD UNIVERSITY PRESS

Trace.

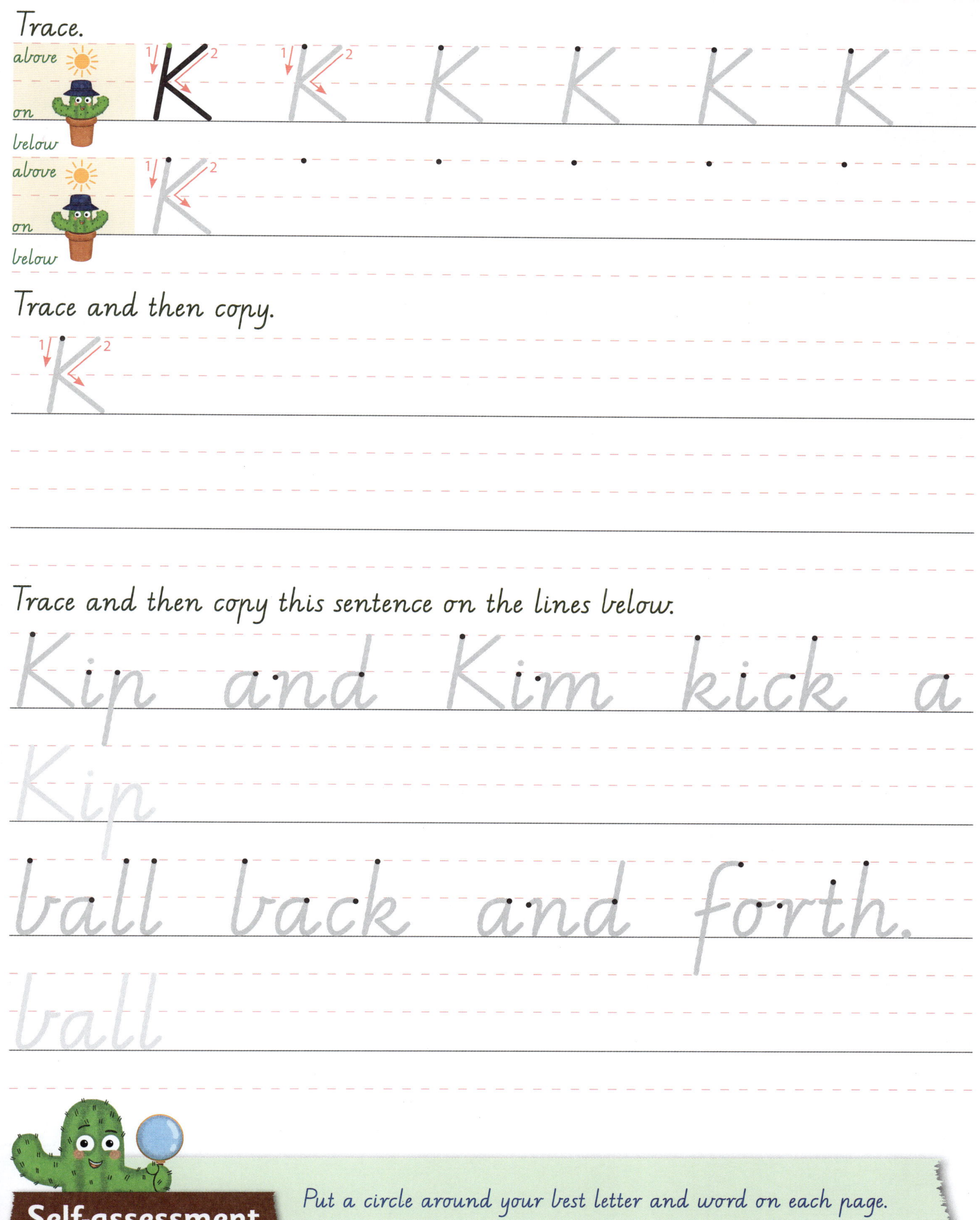

Trace and then copy.

Trace and then copy this sentence on the lines below.

Kip and Kim kick a ball back and forth.

Self-assessment

Put a circle around your best letter and word on each page.
Explain your choice to your teacher or classmate.

Have you checked your posture, pencil grip and paper position?

Have you done your warm-ups?

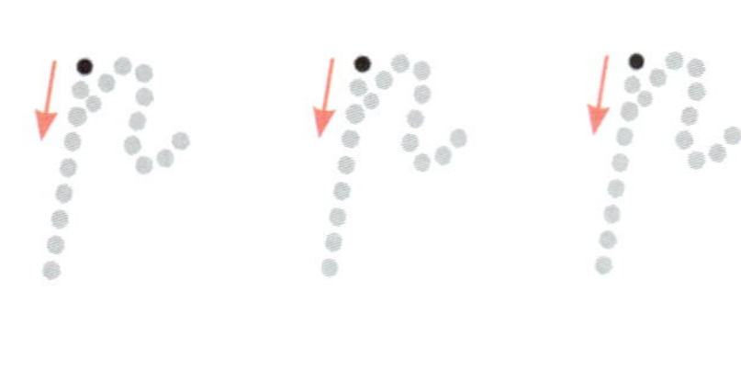

plant

Track, trace and copy the letters and words.

p p p p p p p

p p p p p p p

p

pink pack plant puff

pink

porch power port pip

porch

Trace.

above
on
below

P P P P P P

P

Trace and then copy.

P

Trace and then copy this sentence on the lines below.

Pat went to the pool

Pat

to play and splash.

to

Self-assessment

Put a circle around your best letter and word on each page.
Explain your choice to your teacher or classmate.

Warm-up patterns

Trace the grey lines.

Trace the grey lines.

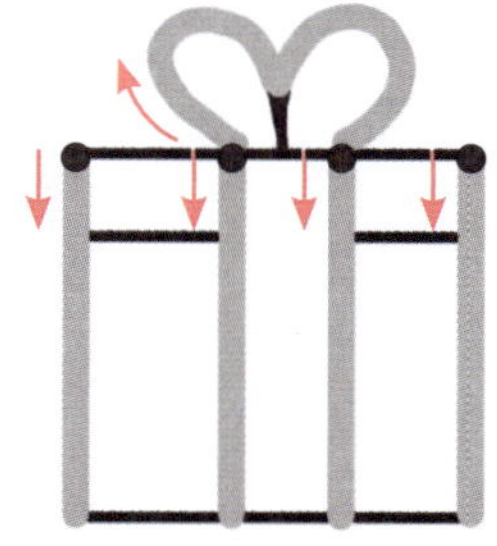
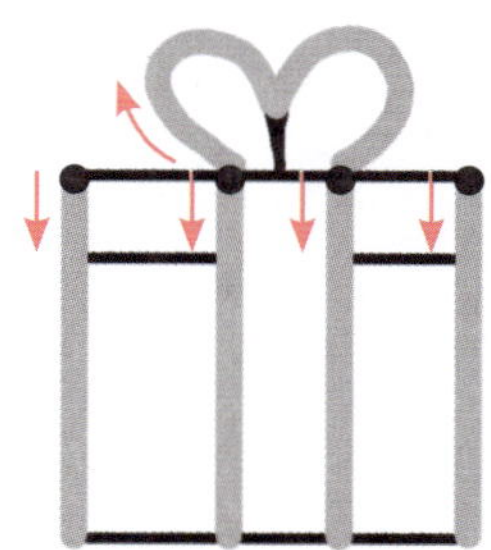
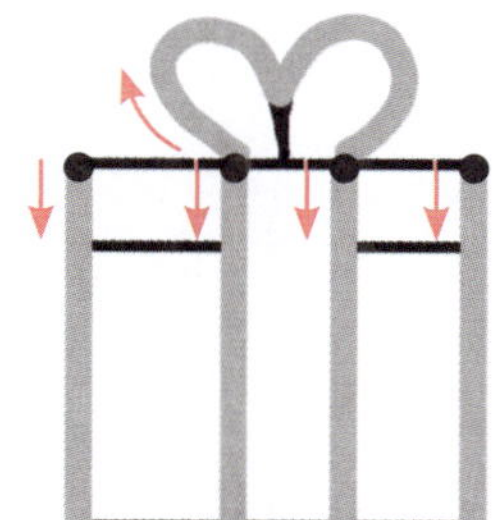
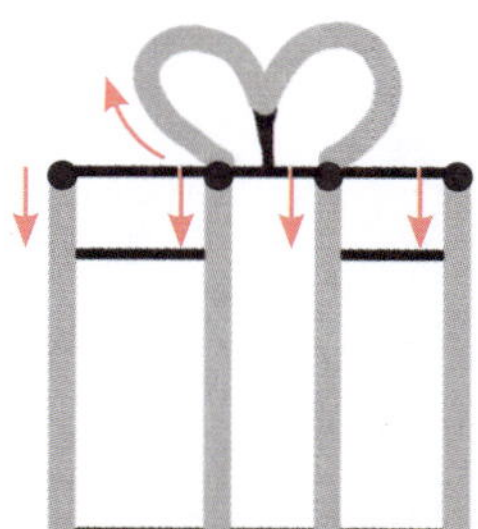

Have you checked your posture, pencil grip and paper position?

Have you done your warm-ups?

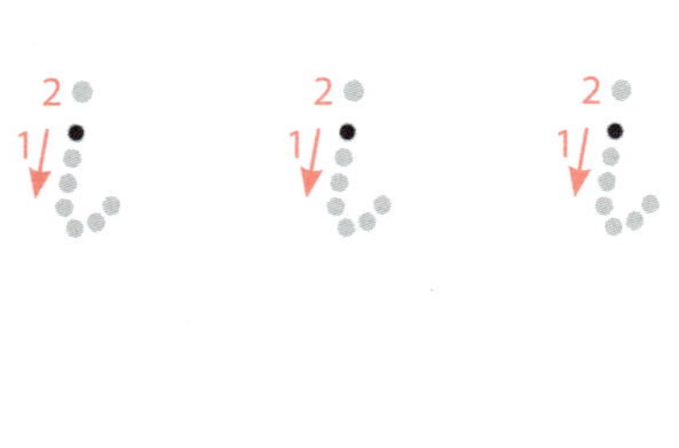

inside

Track, trace and copy the letters and words.

i i i i i i i

i

if it is inside into

if

ill ink in icecream

ill

Trace.

above

on

below

above

on

below

Trace and then copy.

Trace and then copy this sentence on the lines below.

I see a big, bright

I

fish in the pond.

fish

Self-assessment

Put a circle around your best letter and word on each page.
Explain your choice to your teacher or classmate.

Have you checked your posture, pencil grip and paper position?

Have you done your warm-ups?

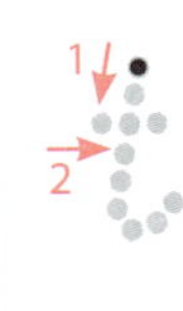

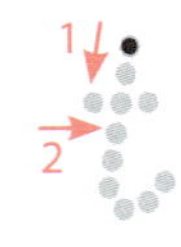

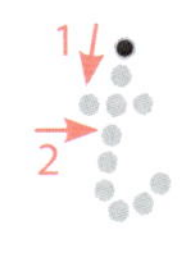

train

Track, trace and copy the letters and words.

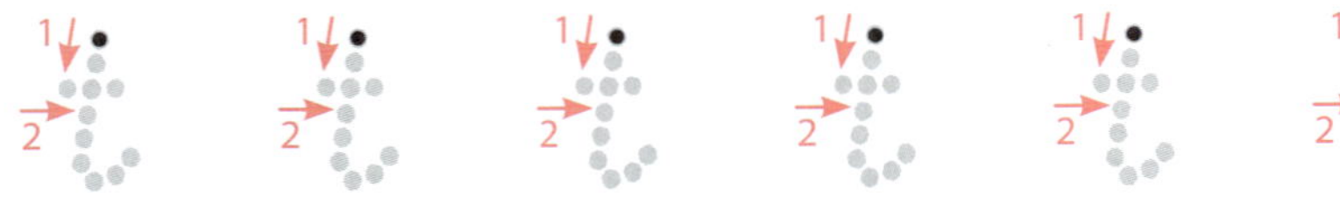

t t t t t t t

t

this them then that

this

tail tank tap thank

tail

OXFORD UNIVERSITY PRESS

Trace.

above
on
below

T T T T T T

above
on
below

T

Trace and then copy.

T

Trace and then copy this sentence on the lines below.

Tess and Tim went into

Tess

town on the train.

town

Self-assessment

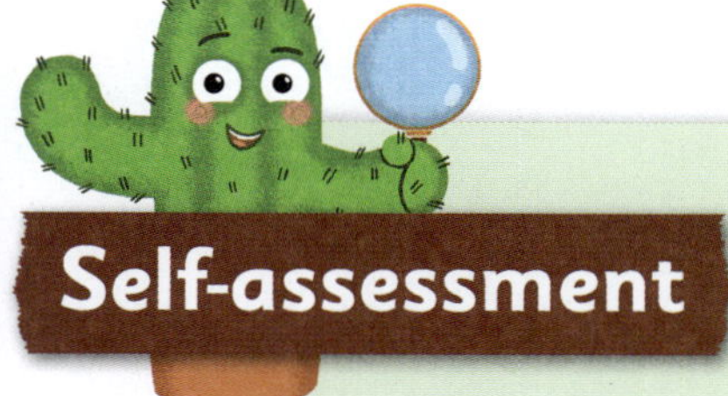

Put a circle around your best letter and word on each page.
Explain your choice to your teacher or classmate.

Have you checked your posture, pencil grip and paper position?

Have you done your warm-ups?

l l l

list

Track, trace and copy the letters and words.

l l l l l l l

l l l l l l l

l

let lid left list loop

let

ladder less letter leg

ladder

Trace.

above

on

below

L L L L L L

above

on

below

L

Trace and then copy.

L

Trace and then copy this sentence on the lines below.

Lee likes a cheese and

Lee

salad roll for lunch.

salad

Self-assessment

Put a circle around your best letter and word on each page.
Explain your choice to your teacher or classmate.

Have you checked your posture, pencil grip and paper position?

Have you done your warm-ups?

jump

Track, trace and copy the letters and words.

j j j j j j j

jog job jets just joke

jog

jacket jam join jaw

jacket

Trace.

above

on

below

j j j j j j

above

on

below

j

Trace and then copy.

j

Trace and then copy this sentence on the lines below.

Jez and Jo jump for

Jez

joy over the jam jars.

joy

Self-assessment

Put a circle around your best letter and word on each page.
Explain your choice to your teacher or classmate.

Have you checked your posture, pencil grip and paper position?

Have you done your warm-ups?

u u u

upset

Track, trace and copy the letters and words.

u u u u u u u

u u u u u u u

u

up us underground

up

underneath upon upset

underneath

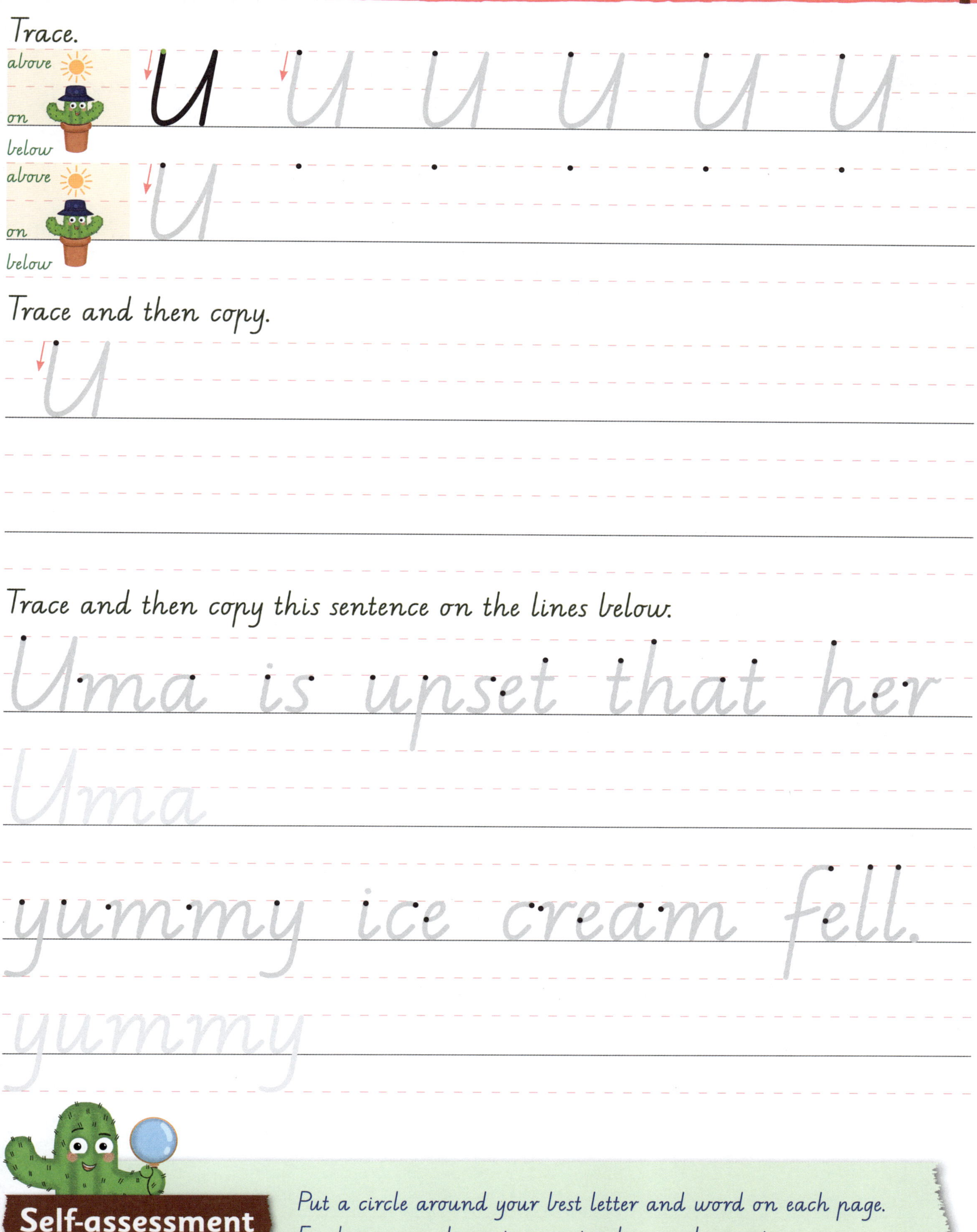

Trace.

above

on

below

U U U U U U

above

on

below

U

Trace and then copy.

U

Trace and then copy this sentence on the lines below.

Uma is upset that her

Uma

yummy ice cream fell.

yummy

Self-assessment

Put a circle around your best letter and word on each page.
Explain your choice to your teacher or classmate.

Have you checked your posture, pencil grip and paper position?

Have you done your warm-ups?

y y y

yawn

Track, trace and copy the letters and words.

y y y y y y y

y y y y y y y

y

yes yap yet yawn

yes

yell yum year yuck

yell

OXFORD UNIVERSITY PRESS

Trace.

Trace and then copy.

Trace and then copy this sentence on the lines below.

Yin said, "I can't find

Yin

my six yellow yaks."

my

Self-assessment

Put a circle around your best letter and word on each page.
Explain your choice to your teacher or classmate.

Have you checked your posture, pencil grip and paper position?

Have you done your warm-ups?

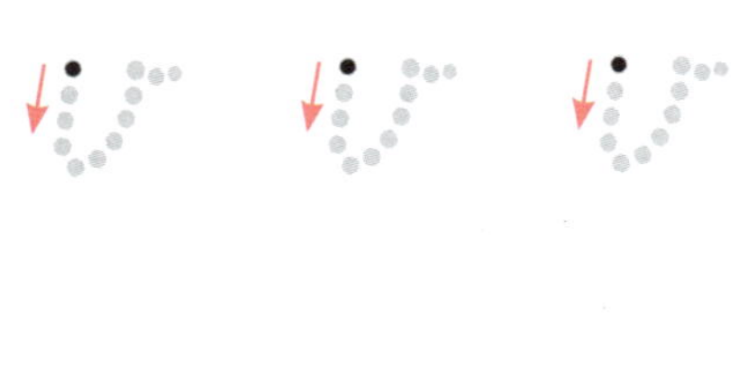

vet

Track, trace and copy the letters and words.

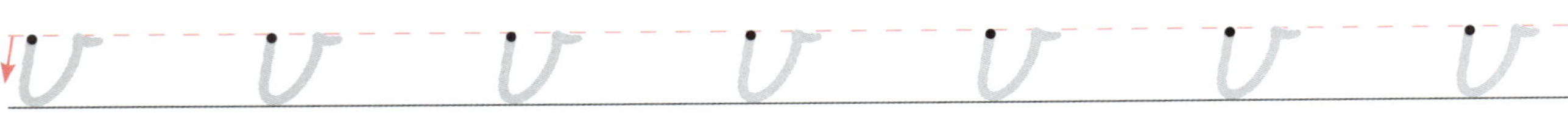

v v v v v v v

v

vet van venue vest void

vet

value volleyball vast

value

Trace.

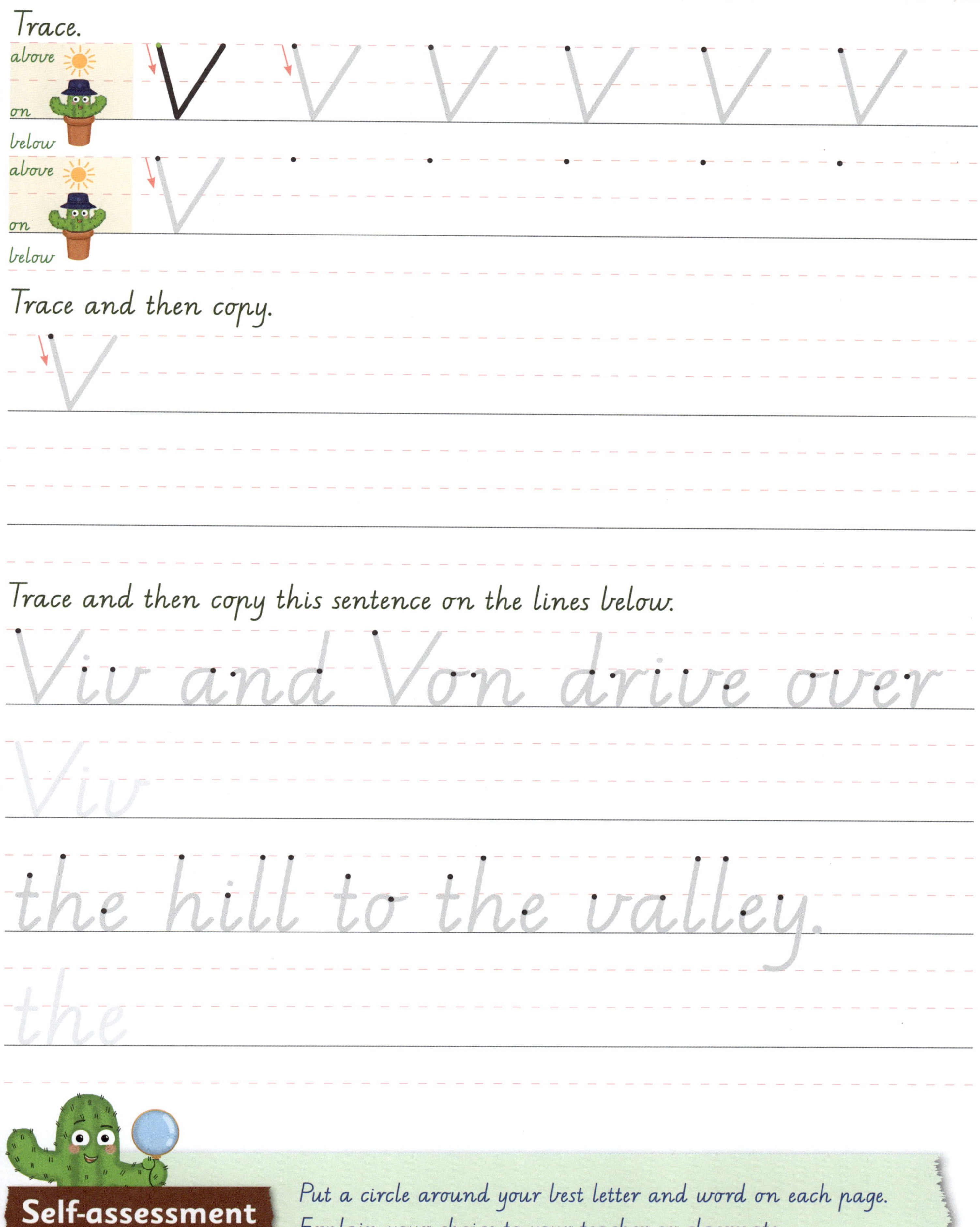

Trace and then copy.

Trace and then copy this sentence on the lines below.

Self-assessment

Put a circle around your best letter and word on each page.
Explain your choice to your teacher or classmate.

Have you checked your posture, pencil grip and paper position?

Have you done your warm-ups?

w w w

wag

Track, trace and copy the letters and words.

w w w w w w w

w w w w w w w

w

wag went wig weep

wag

waiter weed week web

waiter

Trace.

Trace and then copy.

Trace and then copy this sentence on the lines below.

Self-assessment

Put a circle around your best letter and word on each page.
Explain your choice to your teacher or classmate.

Have you checked your posture, pencil grip and paper position?

Have you done your warm-ups?

b b b

bed

Track, trace and copy the letters and words.

b b b b b b b

b b b b b b b

b

but bed back bubble

but

beard big barn bark

beard

Trace.

above

on

below

B B B B B B

above

on

below

B

Trace and then copy.

B

Trace and then copy this sentence on the lines below.

Big and little birds

Big

sit on the bent branch.

sit

Self-assessment

Put a circle around your best letter and word on each page.
Explain your choice to your teacher or classmate.

Numbers

Trace and copy.

1 1

2 2

3 3

4 4

5 5

6 6

7 7

8 8

9 9

10 10

OXFORD UNIVERSITY PRESS

10 10

20 20

30 30

40 40

50 50

60 60

70 70

80 80

90 90

Trace the lower- and upper-case letters.

aA bB cC dD

eE fF gG hH

iI jJ kK lL mM

nN oO pP qQ

rR sS tT uU vV

wW xX yY zZ

Practise any tricky letters below.